...ERMLINE WEST FIFE'S

AMS AND BUSES

WALTER BURT

AMBERLEY

Acknowledgements

Once again, I am indebted to the following people for allowing me to use their fantastic images as an aid to illustrating this book. Without them, the rich variety of images would not exist and would make for some dull and un-interesting reading. In no particular order, my heartfelt thanks go to Robert Dickson; John Sinclair; Paul Redmond; Suzy Scott; Gary Seamarks; Kenneth Barclay; Clair Pendrous; John Connery; Innes Cameron; Barry Sanjana; Robert Clark; John Carter; Christopher Leach; Eddie Taylor; Paul Currie; Len Wright; George Robertson; Bobby Brown Jnr; Mike Penn; Brian Pritchard; David Love; Jo Freeman; Clive A. Brown; Gordon Stirling; John Law and Donald Stewart.

First published 2013

Amberley Publishing
The Hill, Stroud
Gloucestershire, GL5 4EP
www.amberley-books.com

British Library Cataloguing in Publication Data.
A catalogue record for this book is available from the British Library.

ISBN 978 1 4456 1147 1

E-book ISBN: 978 1 4456 1171 6

Typeset in 10pt on 12pt Sabon.
Typesetting and Origination by Amberley Publishing.
Printed in the UK.

Introduction

Let us start this journey a little over 100 years ago when the main mode of travel (out with the railways) was by stagecoach. No, Brian Souter hasn't been running his company that long in Fife; I'm talking about the carriage of fare paying customers. If you could afford it, it was the only way for a lot of people in outlying areas to get from one place to another. A lot of the stagecoach owners operated from the busier areas such as the coastal ports, where they were guaranteed a good business, carrying both passengers and goods.

The Victorian era, just after the turn of the century, was a time of invention and innovation. Great advances were being made in all walks of life and transportation was at the forefront. Electric power, and the invention, and development, of the motor engine ushered in a new era in the transport industry.

With this book, I aim to chart the advances of the trams and buses which have served the people of Dunfermline and West Fife, from the earliest humble motor engined vehicles and electric trams, to the modern day, air conditioned vehicles on the roads at present. I would have liked to have included all vehicular types and the various body manufacturers too. Many have been included in the *Fife Buses* book, and I do not want to merely duplicate images.

I hope that, like my previous two books, the reader enjoys not only the wide selection of vehicles on show, but also takes in the changing face of west Fife, with a lot of changes having taking place in many backgrounds in various locations in the photographs. Many of the images will be unrecognisable to the younger reader, but the older ones might reminisce about something that catches their eye within these pages. As is my practise, I have included number plates, fleet numbers and chassis or body types, while trying to keep it all as simple and uncomplicated as I can, because I know not everyone is a bus enthusiast, but everyone has a memory.

Brief History

Before the introduction of its tram system and early motor buses, Dunfermline was like any other town of similar size the length and breadth of the country. It was reliant on the railways and the local stagecoach owners to move the town's residents from A to B. This was all about to change quite radically. 1909 seemed to be the year that started the ball rolling. It was then that Dunfermline's first motor bus licences were granted, and also the year that the trams started operating.

Kirkcaldy had beaten Dunfermline by six years in the race to be the first town in the Kingdom to operate a tram system. It was seen to be a bit of one-upmanship for the 'Lang town' in the rivalry that has existed for many a year between the two. Dunfermline's tram system, though, would eventually total a mileage of 18.5 miles, beating the combined length of both the Kirkcaldy and Wemyss systems by 4.5 miles, and using a greater amount of tramcars, forty-five compared to the Kirkcaldy and Wemyss combined fleet of thirty-nine.

In 1906, the Fife Tramway Light & Power Company Limited, a subsidiary of the Balfour Beatty organisation, had built an electricity generating station at Townhill, to the north of Dunfermline, for the supply of electricity to the town. The decision was also taken at this time to form another subsidiary company, the Dunfermline & District Traction Company, to operate a tramway system in the town. Parliamentary authority was acquired, and contracts were signed in 1907 for the supply of electricity for the system. Orders were also placed with English company UEC for the construction of the tramcars.

Like the other two tramway systems in Fife, covered in *Kirkcaldy and Central Fife's Trams and Buses*, Dunfermline's system was built to a gauge of 3 feet 6 inches. The first section, completed in 1909 (but not the first in operation), was the section from Townhill, naturally, as that was where the power was to come from, to East Port in Dunfermline. Simultaneously, a line was constructed from East Port to Cowdenbeath and was opened on 2 November that year. The Townhill branch opened the following day. Lochgelly was reached and made operational just before Christmas that year, and Kelty was reached in November 1910 via a branch from Cowdenbeath at the aptly named Junction Road. Another two years passed before the system reached its north-easterly limit at Lochore in December 1912. Another short branch opened just over a year later when the system was extended a short distance west to Rumblingwell. The final extension was completed in May 1918, when the line reached its southern extent at the new Rosyth Dockyard. It does seem a bit like closing the stable door after the horse has bolted, as the Great War was almost over by then.

During the early planning stages of the tram routes, Kelty was to have been reached via a junction at the top of Kingseathill on the Townhill branch, but as mentioned, this was changed and the town was reached via Cowdenbeath. A line to

Inverkeithing was authorised but never built, after a lot of the preparatory work had been carried out. This is evident in the wideness of Queensferry Road in Rosyth, a part of the route which it was to take. At one time, it was also intended to construct a tramway between Lochgelly and Kirkcaldy, and a Parliamentary Bill was passed and authorised for this purpose. If this proposal had indeed happened, an unbroken line of tramways would have existed for over thirty miles between Rosyth and Leven.

The Dunfermline & District Traction Company operated double-decked tramcars of the open-top type, necessitated by the many railway overbridges on the tram lines operated. Only two single-deck cars were used by the company, those being 44 and 45, the two Brush-built cars that were acquired from the Wemyss Tramways Company in 1932, when their system closed

The author Alan Brotchie informs us that the livery for the Dunfermline tramway system was 'Bright Green and Cream'. In relatively recent times, two buses have been repainted into representations of what Bright Green looks like. The first one was a Volvo Citybus, C793 USG (FRA 93), as operated by Fife Scottish in 1987. It was repainted to commemorate the fiftieth anniversary of the last day of the trams. A photograph can be seen in this book, as well as in the *Fife Buses* book by the same author and publisher. The second one was a low floor single-deck MAN and was operated on service no. 19 to commemorate the 100th anniversary of the route between Dunfermline and Cowdenbeath, and it too can be seen within these pages. You will see two completely different shades of green when you compare the images.

You will also see within this book photographs of typical uniforms as worn by the members of staff. A copy of the *Dunfermline Press* from January 1996 carries an article about Ernie Mitchell, a former tram driver, who had just passed away. It was in fact he who was the driver of the last tramcar in service from Dunfermline to Rosyth Dockyard, returning empty to leave the car at Hill of Beath – the final resting place for the tramcar fleet. In it, he had recalled about how, in winter times, the drivers used to wear clogs to help keep their feet warm, and how they would wear several layers of clothing underneath a greatcoat and a raincoat (A greatcoat is like a trench coat). I was also intrigued by his memory of the drivers carrying potatoes in their pockets to clean dirty windows in the tramcars. Also in the winter months, it was the tram drivers who used to sand the tracks, especially on Townhill Road, and it was often due to this that the road was kept open.

Much like how the buses work nowadays, extra tramcars were put on at peak periods such as football match days, workers travelling to and from work (these were mostly miners in those early days), or even private hires.

Accidents were, luckily, few and far between, although a minor accident occurred just after 5 p.m. on 24 May 1932, as reported in the *Dunfermline Press* of the day. A passenger had an alarming experience in a tramcar travelling from Rumblingwell to Townhill. At the junction of Grieve Street and Chalmers Street, the tramcar had been stopped to allow the passage of a car. When it restarted, the tramcar left the rails and the front canopy collided with the wall of the premises on the east side of Chalmers Street occupied by Wm Cunningham & Co. (Dunfermline), Ltd. One of the factory windows was broken, and the canopy of the tramcar was slightly damaged. No one was injured.

Although the first motor buses had been licensed in Dunfermline in 1909 as well, it was not until the First World War had ended that the motor bus really started to make a difference in the area. They were becoming more reliable due to advances in technology, and more readily available too as post-war chassis were now surplus to War Department use. A few early entrepreneurial newcomers had started running competing services on the wealthy tram routes, and a few ran services to the outlying areas around the region such as Charlestown, Culross, Aberdour, Burntisland, Saline… the list goes on. Similarly to what happened in Kirkcaldy, many of the new operators folded, or were absorbed by larger operators. Many operators weathered the storm of the early years and prospered and went on to provide good services until they too were absorbed by larger companies. In 1924, as a result of over indulgence by the small operators on the tram routes, the Dunfermline & District Tramway Company decided to operate its own bus services in competition with the small operators. A sizable fleet was used by the 'Tram-Bus Company' to eventually oust the small pirate companies on the tram routes. In 1926, the bus department of the tram company was effectively taken over by the Scottish General Omnibus Company. The SGO was also a part of the Fife Tramway Light & Power Company. In 1930, the SGO and all its subsidiary companies were purchased in the name of W. Alexander & Sons. Among the other operators that were to grow were A. & R. Forrester of Lochgelly, and Simpson's Motor Services of Dunfermline. These two amalgamated in 1929 to create one of the largest undertakings in Fife. The result was Simpson's & Forrester's, a company that was an associate of Walter Alexander, and was used by Alexander's as the west Fife operator of the Scottish Bus Group.

The various liveries used by the main operators mentioned in this book were as follows. As previously mentioned, the Dunfermline & District Traction Company colours were bright green and cream. The Tram-Bus vehicles were dark red and cream, similar to the Wemyss tramways buses further up the coast. A. & R. Forrester's vehicles were crimson red and cream, while the livery of their counterparts at Simpson's Motor Services is unknown. The combined company would later adopt Alexander's blue livery, which would remain from when Alexander's took full control until the Alexander empire split in 1961. Most other operators have been covered in other, more detailed publications by Alan Brotchie.

Between 1962 and 1991, Fife's vehicles remained in the much loved red and cream livery. The same colours remained even when the company, by this time known as 'Fife Scottish', started to adopt the 'large logo' scheme in the mid-1980s, which was basically more cream and less red. It all changed again from 1991, when Stagecoach bought the Fife Scottish company after the introduction of privatisation. Stagecoach started to repaint the buses in their own 'stripy' or 'candy stripe' livery. Stagecoach changed their identity once more around 2002, and it is this 'swirl' livery that is still around on the buses operated by Stagecoach in Fife at present.

Many of the routes operating in west Fife have changed little over the last century, including (unfortunately) the running times. There have also been numerous new routes created and a lot of them have been recent additions as the town of Dunfermline has now called itself a city, and is rapidly growing and seems to be turning into an extension of Edinburgh. Dunfermline has always been ideally located within the central belt, and is within easy reach of the major towns and cities within central Scotland.

Bus depots used at present by companies running services can be found at Cowdenbeath and Dunfermline, the principal town in the area. Rennies of Dunfermline, now part of the Stagecoach group, operate from a depot at Wellwood, to the north of Dunfermline. There have been rumours circulating in the past regarding a 'super depot' for the area, and I believe that it may happen one day, as the local depots are bursting at the seams with tri-axle vehicles – watch this space.

A horse-drawn carriage can be seen under the start of the overhead tram wires in this image showing the east end of Dunfermline High Street. This was before the tramway extended down the High Street on the route to Rumblingwell, to the north-west of the town. Notice how busy the scene looks, even though this is almost 100 years ago.

This image was taken at the extreme east end of the High Street and shows tramcar number 2 adjacent to 'Porter's East Port Bar' in the East Port itself. It is heading east, showing Townhill as its destination. Although a lot of the buildings have changed since this was taken, the distinctive frontage of the East Port Bar still looks the same today.

A side view of an original tramcar shows the layout as delivered to the Traction Company. They would later require an additional level to the safety railings around the top deck of the cars. The image also shows the tramcar with a full load of women passengers – perhaps an outing of sorts?

Tramcar number 4 makes light work of a return trip to Dunfermline as it trundles through Cowdenbeath High Street. The latticework on the overhead line gantry posts was quite distinctive and can be seen to good effect in this image. No other motor vehicles can be seen, but there is an abundance of horse-drawn carts and wagons on show.

A well-known postcard depicting tramcar number 11 as it sits at the terminal point at Dunfermline High Street. It had just arrived from the west as the arm is still in the trailing position. A dog is seen standing in front of the tramcar, blissfully unaware of the tramcar's presence. Colourised postcards showed the tramcars as being a deep brown colour. The Dunfermline & District colours were green and cream.

Side-by-side images showing track movements that disrupted the tram services. On the left, tramcar number 13 is impeded by the severe misalignment to one of the rails as it travels to Rumblingwell in Dunfermline. On the right, tramcar number 22 is inconvenienced by the works as it heads down the reserved track on a run to Kelty.

Townhill is the location here as we see tramcar number 24 slowly arriving at the terminal point in the mining village. The cars terminated outside what was then the co-op building on the Main Street. Although many of the buildings have changed, the scene is still pretty much recognisable.

The tramcars always seemed to attract the crowds, especially children, as seen here as tramcar number 3 rounds the bend at Cowdenbeath Fountain. Once one of the best-known institutions in Fife, Dicks Co-operative Society's Cowdenbeath store can be seen in the background Notice how muddy and uneven the road surface is when heavily used and after a downpour.

Tramcar number 24 has just trundled round the corner from Bank Street in Lochgelly and is making steady progress on the run to Dunfermline. As shown in other images, tramcars attract the crowds, usually younger children as they were still a bit of a novelty when first introduced.

This rather grainy looking image shows what in effect turned out to be Scotland's first dual carriageway. It is situated on the stretch of road between Rosyth Halt railway station and the Cottage Inn public house, in Dunfermline. This area is adjacent to the Pitcorthie housing scheme on the right, and the former Solectron factory on the left, and still remains recognisable to this day.

Lower Oakfield – Kelty

A view of the tram lines at Oakfield, looking away from the terminus at Kelty Cross. Kelty bus depot would eventually be built in this area, behind the photographer and to the right. This photograph would appear to have been taken at a time near the end of the trams' working lives as no overhead wires seem to be present.

Looking in the opposite direction from the previous image, but taken from approximately the same location, we can see the terminus for tramcars just beyond the crossroads in Kelty. Surprisingly little has changed in the area. The buildings on the right are still there, while the left-hand buildings have been replaced, but the area is still largely recognisable today.

Tramcar number 6 was a unique vehicle in that it was the only one in the fleet to be enclosed around the driving areas. This was the one that the 'Motormen', as the tramcar drivers were called, used to pray to get during the autumn and winter as it offered a degree of comfort in the cold months. It is seen heading down the New Row, past the Alhambra, on a run to Rosyth Dockyard. As can be seen by the posters on display, Laurel and Hardy films were very much the order of the day.

The Cowdenbeath tramcar depot was a sizeable building, and although the depot will still be recognisable, the frontage to the shed has changed almost beyond recognition. All that remains from the original depot are the workshop offices on the left-hand side of the image. It is now the home for buses used by its present occupier, Stagecoach Fife Buses.

Bridge Street, Dunfermline

Dunfermline's Bridge Street is the location of this early colourised postcard image, which shows tramcars heading in opposite directions near the present day Glen Gates. As I noticed when compiling the *Kirkcaldy and Central Fife's Trams and Buses* book, the people that coloured the postcards tended to depict them in a rather bland varnished dark wood colour. We know our trams were green and cream, but there is a little bit of debate as to the exact shade of green used.

An original photograph shows tramcar number 29 making light work of the journey up the New Row to Dunfermline town centre. This is the junction between the New Row, Comely Park in the background and, behind the photographer, Priory Lane. It will be noted that the tramcar has come from Rosyth Dockyard and is therefore busy with naval personnel.

Another side view of one of the Dunfermline & District Traction Company tramcars, showing the additional height to the guard rail around the upper deck of the refurbished car and the lowered destination box. This image also shows the style in which the company name was applied, on the lower right panel of each side of the vehicles.

Glencraig is the location shown here, with one of the company tramcars heading along the main thoroughfare after a downpour. We know this due to the puddles of water where the kerb would be, on the right-hand side of the tracks. What is most notable to the author is the excellent condition of the brick setts on the surrounding roadway when compared to other images, in which the road can only be described as a mucky track.

A rather fine image showing tramcar number 38 seemingly posed for the photographer. The location is Bank Street in Lochgelly, and the tramcar will be heading for Dunfermline once the tramcar crew rejoin their vehicle. Another good view of the new, lowered position of the destination box.

This image depicts one of the Dunfermline & District tramcars stuck fast in a snowdrift at an unspecified location on one of the routes. The 'motorman' can be seen at the controls, while another poor soul, perhaps the conductor, tries to help dig the tramcar out of trouble. Winters must have been quite harsh for the tramcar crews.

A rather lovely image showing two of the tramcars at the terminus at the west end of the East Port in Dunfermline. Most of the buildings in this view have been demolished or replaced, but, as you will notice in most of the photographs in these pages, the locations remain largely identifiable. The tramcar in front of the photograph, number 12, has Townhill as its destination. The unknown tramcar behind must be destined for Lochore.

Tramcar number 16 is seen trundling along the East Port in Dunfermline heading eastwards, with Lochgelly displayed on its destination equipment. Much has changed on the north side of East Port, on the left of the picture, while the churches and other buildings on the right appear to look much as they are today.

A rare evening photograph shows tramcar number 2 making its way down Bridge Street in Dunfermline. Although not showing much of the tramcar as such, this image has been included to display the luminescence given off by the single large headlight on these vehicles. The tramcar was heading towards Rumblingwell, the terminus to the west of the town centre.

The left image shows tramcar conductress Ina Sharp on the step of one of the un-refurbished cars, wearing the typical company uniform. The right-hand image shows Ina again, along side tramcar driver, or 'motorman' as they were known, John Anderson. Ina is again wearing the typical conductress attire, while John is seen in typical motorman uniform with white cap cover on his hat. They are on the step of a refurbished tramcar in this view. John and Ina eventually married. (*John Connery Collection*)

John Anderson is shown here again, on the left, wearing the typical motorman uniform without white cap cover. The jacket is a double breasted design more akin to a military uniform. He is shown again on the right, after the trams ceased running, wearing his new uniform from Walter Alexander in his new role as a bus driver. (*John Connery Collection*)

John Anderson is still the subject here, as we see him further on in years with his shift bus and a new conductress. Bus crews, as with the tramcar crews, worked with the same people, in some cases, for most of their lives. Relationships happened in Fife, as elsewhere, and a lot of people like John and Ina lived happily because of it. (*John Connery Collection*)

The arrival of the buses signalled that the final nail was almost in the coffin lid for the tramway system. Tramcar 26 sits beside one of the replacement buses at St Leonards depot in Dunfermline. New in 1937, WG 5255 (R 147) was a Leyland TD4 with Leyland's own bodywork and served with Walter Alexander until it was scrapped by the company in 1959.

Hill of Beath was the final resting place for the Dunfermline & District tramcars when they ceased running on 4 July 1937. The long line up of cars can be seen here, including the two 8-wheeled, single-deck vehicles inherited from the Wemyss Traction Company in 1932.

An official posed photograph from the Albion Company shows Valkerie Model FG 3828, number 13 in the fleet of its new owners, Simpson's Motor Service of Dunfermline. New in 1928, it would retain the same fleet number when Simpson's combined with A. & R. Forrester of Lochgelly to operate as the West Fife area of operations for Walter Alexander.

Seen within the confines of the bus shed, at the combined tram and bus depot at Dunfermline St Leonards, four Tilling-Stevens vehicles are in various stages of readiness for their day's work. The vehicle at the rear is using solid tyres while the others are all using the new pneumatic ones.

Not the clearest of images, but this postcard dated from 1937 shows a variety of buses on the newly opened Glen Bridge, Dunfermline. The vehicles, although seemingly in different colour schemes, are all believed to be those of the principal local operator, Walter Alexander.

Walter Alexander relied on the robust Leyland Titan, which was, for many of the early years, the principal double-decker in the Alexander fleet. This Leyland TD3, AWB 929 (R611), is seen resting between duties at its home depot at Dunfermline St Leonards. This vehicle never made it into service by the time the Alexander empire split into the three operating areas in 1961. (*Innes Cameron collection*)

Typical of the Walter Alexander fleet from the mid-1930s, we see all-Leyland TD4 WG 4935 (R133) sitting in the yard at its home depot of Dunfermline. New in 1937, this vehicle made it into the Alexander (Fife) fleet at the split in 1961. It was, however, withdrawn the following year and scrapped by Muir's of Kirkcaldy. (*Innes Cameron collection*)

A very official-looking photograph shown here of some of the conductresses, drivers and inspectors at the Kelty depot of Walter Alexander's. The staff look almost military like in their appearance while wearing enough paraphernalia to make a modern-day collector wish for a time machine.

WG 8259 (R240) was a Leyland TD5 with Leyland's own bodywork. It was new in 1939 and lasted with Walter Alexander until the company split into the three operating areas in 1961, making the vehicle twenty-two years old. It was sold on to a dealership in Glasgow. Close examination of the depot shed code plate reveals that the bus was one allocated to Dunfermline Market Street (D2). (*Robert Dickson Collection*)

Seen sitting at the drop-off area at St Margaret's Street bus stance, Dunfermline, we find DWG909 (RB153), an Alexander-bodied Leyland PD2/12 from 1953. It is being used on service 300, which in the 1950s ran from the St Margaret's bus stance to North Queensferry via Rosyth Crossroads and Inverkeithing. This vehicle lasted until withdrawal in 1970 and was subsequently sold to Muir's of Kirkcaldy. (*Robert Dickson Collection*)

This photograph shows AMS 216 (RO509), a Cowdenbeath depot Guy Arab 2 with Northern Counties bodywork, in a bit of trouble in 1958 when it left the road and got stuck in a ditch while enroute to Ballingry. New in 1945, it was eventually withdrawn in 1968 and was sold to Muir's in Kirkcaldy the following year. Muir's used it as a seat store until 1974 when it was decided to break it up for scrap. (*Eddie Taylor Collection*)

Seen here at its home depot of Lochgelly, Guy Arab 2 AMS 317 (RO542) saw twenty years' service with Alexander's in Fife. New in 1945 to Walter Alexander, this Weymann-bodied example ended its working life with Alexander's (Fife) in 1965 and was sold on for scrap to Dunsmore of Larkhall. The ribbed effect of the Weymann roof panels can be clearly seen in this image, taken at the turn of the 1960s. (*John Sinclair*)

GYL 381 (RO633) was one of seven Guy Arab 2s acquired from London Transport in 1951. This vehicle was new in August 1945, with bodywork by Northern Counties, and served in the Fife fleet until March 1963, when it was sold on to Horne, a dealership in Denny. It is seen here parked up near the promenade in Kirkcaldy alongside BMS 591 (G69), a Massey-bodied Guy Arab 3 single-decker. (*John Sinclair*)

AMS 159 (RO487) was another Guy Arab 2 with a Northern Counties body. Seen here within the confines of Cowdenbeath depot, this image shows to good effect the 'armadillo' look to the rear of the roof caused by the folding of the aluminium sheet to create the rear curved dome. Another long-serving vehicle dating from 1944, it was withdrawn in 1965 and sold on to Dunsmore in Larkhall. (*John Sinclair*)

CWG 342 (PA215) was a 1950 Leyland PS1, with the rather distinctive Burlingham Body work. It seems to be the odd one out as its stable mates have all received the new Ayres red livery that was being applied from 1962. In 1964 it was converted to a towing vehicle, before being sold the following year to the Civil Defence. All the vehicles are parked up near Kirkcaldy depot, having been on football specials to Kirkcaldy from the west of Fife. One of the floodlight pylons of Starks Park can be seen in the background. (*John Sinclair*)

Northern Counties-bodied Guy Arab 2 AMS 314 (RO539) is seen sitting in the recently extended yard space at the rear of Dunfermline depot in this 1962 photograph. Compare the traditional old blue livery with the newer, more vibrant Ayres red livery applied to the Guy Arab in the background. (*John Sinclair*)

All-Leyland PD2/1 CWG 296 (RB102) sits within the confines of Dunfermline St Leonards depot in 1962, awaiting its next turn of duty for the day. Beside it, and undergoing a bit of side panel restoration work, is Bristol LD6G Lodekka GWG977 (FRD1), Fife's first Lodekka, which arrived in May 1956. Both vehicles were withdrawn in 1971, with FRD1 ending up at Muir's in Kirkcaldy. I have no record of what happened to RB102. (*John Sinclair*)

Two Cravens-bodied Guy Arab 3s stand side by side at Dunfermline depot in 1962 to show the similarity in the cream relief bands and other black and yellow lining when the livery changed. The new red was a straight swap for the previous blue. Both of these buses were new in 1948 and would both be withdrawn twenty-two years later, in 1970. They stayed together when sold to a dealer in Preston the same year. (*John Sinclair*)

Kirkcaldy is the location of Lochgelly depot's Bristol LS6G, FWG 842 (E7), as it makes a pick-up of passengers returning to its hometown via Bowhill. The bluebird emblem was a prominent feature on the coaches of Walter Alexander, but as the years rolled on, the Fife company slowly dropped its use, leaving the Northern and Midland areas to eventually both claim usage, even after privatisation. (*John Sinclair*)

Alexander-bodied Leyland PD2/12 DWG 907 (RB151) is flanked by a couple of Northern Counties-bodied Guy Arab 2s, in the shape of GYL 307 (RO631) on the left, and AMS 213 (RO506) to its right. The two Guy Arabs may be from the same year (1945) but they sport some minor differences in body work. They were both withdrawn in 1963. The Leyland was a 1953 build and lasted until withdrawn, late in 1971. (*John Sinclair*)

Dunfermline Abbey is quite an imposing backdrop to KWG 611 (RD58), an LD6G Lodekka, seen here at rest in the St Margaret's Street bus stance (the lower stance). It has just arrived, and reversed into the stance, after a run from Rosyth Dockyard, at one time the busiest single site employer in Scotland. (*Robert Dickson Collection*)

The difference between 'lowbridge' and 'highbridge' body styles is plain to see in this image of Guy Arab 2 CST 5 (FRO574), with bodywork by Northern Counties, and Guy Arab 3 AWG 372 (FRO586), with body work by Cravens. Also clear to see are the differences in application of cream relief bands between the two models. (*John Sinclair*)

Leyland PD1 CCS 407 (FRB163), with an Eastern Coach Works body, is seen making a reversing manoeuvre at Lochgelly depot in 1968. It had been on loan to Fife from Western SMT in August 1966, but was acquired outright the following year. It never lasted long though, being withdrawn and sent to Muir's scrapyard in May 1970 following an accident in December 1969. (*John Sinclair*)

Guy Arab 2 AMS 154 (FRO482) with Northern Counties body work is seen making haste on a private outing in the mid-1960s. It is at an undisclosed location with a full load, and may in fact be on an Omnibus Society outing. (*John Sinclair*)

Seen at the rear of Carnegie Drive bus station, DMS 830 (FPB17) was a Dunfermline-based Leyland OPS2/1 with Alexander body work which was new in 1951. It was converted to PS1 standard in 1960 by the transfer of parts from withdrawn PS1s. It was withdrawn in 1967 and sold, like many other vehicles at the time, to the graveyard known as Muir's of Kirkcaldy. (*John Sinclair*)

Cowdenbeath depot is the location of this single-decked Guy Arab 3, AMS 580 (FG50) with a body by Brockhouse. It was the transitional period just after 1962, as a blue-liveried Guy Arab can be seen behind. FG50 was getting ready to do a run to Comrie Colliery, further to the west past Dunfermline. The west of Fife was a fairly industrious area regarding mining, and was hit hard by the closures during the 1980s after the disastrous strike action of the time. (*John Sinclair*)

During the middle part of last century, it was not uncommon to find local operators providing buses and coaches for exclusive use on tours. Meldrum & Dawson, who had premises in St Margaret's Street, Dunfermline, was one such company, and one of their Duple-bodied Bedford OBs, FSP327, is seen here in the presence of co-owner Douglas Meldrum. (*Paul Currie*)

XOV 7 was a strange-looking beast which Rennies acquired in 1963 from Castle Coaches of Birmingham. It was a Guy Warrior with a Mulliner forty-one-seat coach body and a central entrance door. It is pictured here on Main Street, Cairneyhill, near to the main depot entrance. (*John Sinclair*)

ORV 986 was a Leyland PD2/40 with Metro-Cammell bodywork, new in 1958 to Portsmouth as their fleet number 109. It ended up with Rennies during the late 1960s and is seen here among the company of other Leyland half-cabs. Photographed on 5 May 1974, this was the yellow livery used by Rennies in the early 1970s for their double-decker vehicles. (*Barry Sanjana*)

Two old, well-known establishments, the Bath Tavern and the Belleville Hotel, can be seen in Pilmuir Street, from where Leyland PD2/3 DMS 502 (FRB142) can be seen turning. This Alexander-bodied vehicle was new in 1951 and gave twenty years' service to the people of Fife, being withdrawn and sold to Muir's scrapyard in 1971. (*Robert Dickson Collection*)

Service lorry FG 9432 (185) rests at the rear of Dunfermline depot sometime during the early 1960s. It started life with Simpson's & Forrester's as an Alexander-bodied Leyland LT5B and was acquired by Alexander's in 1938. It was withdrawn and had the body scrapped in 1955, the chassis being used as a service lorry using the body from L173. It was transferred to Alexander (Fife) in 1961, withdrawn in 1965 and sold to Muir's in Kirkcaldy for scrapping. (*John Sinclair*)

A quintet of conductresses is seen here sharing a happy moment in the yard at Dunfermline St Leonards depot sometime during the 1960s. In the background can be seen one of the Bedford VAS1 buses operated by Alexander (Fife) at the time.

Guy Arab 3 AWG378 (FRO592) is sitting beside the 'school wall' at Dunfermline Depot. The school referred to is St Leonards Primary School, situated just over the wall. The other building in the background is an annexed part of the Dunfermline High School. A sturdy-looking chap in overalls can also be seen beside the often pictured, but never noticed, telephone pole near the depot entrance. One of three poles, it is still there to this day. (*Len Wright*)

Leyland PD2/1 CWG 44 (FRB66), with Alexander body work, sits at the rear of Dunfermline depot, awaiting its next turn out on the road. It was new in 1950, and is beside stable mate CWG 296 (RB102), an all-Leyland vehicle, also new in 1950. The difference in body styles is very apparent in this photograph, with the Leyland vehicle displaying a neater style of body. Both vehicles were withdrawn and sold to Muir's for scrapping in 1971. (*Paul Redmond*)

As seen in a previous image, Leyland PD1 CCS 407 (FRB163), a purchase from Western SMT in 1967, fits in well at its new home at Lochgelly depot on 16 April that year. The clean lines of the Eastern Coach Works body make it look very Lodekka-like in appearance, apart from the cab area. (*John Sinclair*)

Dunfermline depot is the location, just outside the workshop entrance, as a member of the engineering staff makes an adjustment to BMS 857 (FG87), a 1948 Guy Arab 3 single-decker with body work by Guy themselves. The other building in the background belonged to the AMS (Alexander Motor Services) social club, but is now demolished. (*Robert Dickson Collection*)

Stuck fast below the low railway bridge in Harbour Place, Burntisland, we see Cravens-bodied Guy Arab 3 AWG 384 (FRO598). It came to grief in 1964 after an inexperienced driver was unaware of a height restriction on this bridge while going off route. The vehicle was withdrawn as a result, but the chassis was put to good use, as can be seen in the following photograph. (*George Robertson Collection*)

This was the result of the previous image. AWG 384 became towing vehicle L7 from December 1964. It ran on trade plate A17 AXA and ended up being sold to Muir's in Kirkcaldy in 1975. It was, however, reported as still being at Gallatown works the following year, but this may have been about the time that Muir's bought the works at Gallatown, which was also the former tram depot. More can be read about this in *Kirkcaldy and Central Fife's Trams and Buses*. (*John Sinclair*)

Alexander-bodied Leyland OPS2/1 DMS 832 (FPB19) is parked up at the fuel pump at Dunfermline depot on a lovely summer day in 1968. A couple of young lads, one with a camera in hand, can be seen on the left. Again, this was perhaps part of an Omnibus Society tour, which were quite common at one time. Depot rules and regulations were more relaxed than they are nowadays. (*John Sinclair*)

I included a similar photograph to this in the first book about Fife Buses from the 1960s to the 1990s, showing a Lodekka, KWG612 (FRD59), in the background. This image depicts Bristol LS6G FWG847 (FE12) travelling along the same, much-changed street, in Dunfermline. These buildings at St Leonards no longer exist and the area is much more open, with large grassed areas on both sides of the road. (*Len Wright*)

In my humble opinion, the Alexander (Fife) Ayres red colour really suited this type of vehicle and also, I thought, was quite pleasing to the eye. Alexander-bodied Leyland PS1 BWG 308 (FPA82) wears it well when photographed at its home depot in Lochgelly on 11 September 1964. New in 1948, it was withdrawn in 1969 and sold to Muir's in Kirkcaldy. Later the same year, it was working with a contractor, Jamieson, at the Forth Bridge. (*John Sinclair*)

FPA82 is seen again in September 1964, but in the company of JWG 506 (FGA15), a relatively new Alexander-bodied Guy Arab LUF, only six years old at the time. It would, however, only last another eight years, as in December of 1972 it took the familiar road to Kirkcaldy, to the graveyard for Fife's buses at Muir's scrapyard. (*John Sinclair*)

HXA 401E (FRD201), an FLF-type Lodekka, makes its way past the Carnegie swimming pool in Pilmuir Street, Dunfermline, on an unknown working. The route number is showing 5, which was a service from St Margaret's bus stance to Rosyth. The junction area in the photograph has changed quite radically, but the buildings remain basically the same, only missing the recent additions to the swimming pool. (*Robert Dickson Collection*)

One of the first buses to be ordered after the 1961 split was 7402 SP (FRD154), an FLF-type Lodekka which arrived new in 1962. It is the only colour image I have seen of an FLF type in full livery, complete with yellow panel lining, and is seen having just arrived at a strangely quiet Carnegie Drive bus stance on 7 July 1962. (*John Sinclair*)

There were five Albion Victor FT3AB buses, dating from 1950, in Walter Alexander's fleet which served their entire working lives in Fife. This one, CWG 229 (FBA4), is from Cowdenbeath depot and is seen parked up in the depot yard, ready to go out on one of Fife's popular tours. This vehicle was withdrawn in 1964, but ended up with the Phoenix Club for the Disabled in Inverkeithing the same year. (*John Sinclair*)

A nice photograph of one of the ugly ducklings. The Alexander-bodied Lowlander was not the prettiest body design by Alexander's and tended to make the whole thing look hideously out of proportion. 7417 SP (FRE4) was a Cowdenbeath-allocated vehicle and was being used on the 314 service between Dunfermline and Ballingry, the forerunner to the current service 19. (*John Sinclair*)

When the Forth Road Bridge was opened by the Queen in 1964, the first official bus journey to make its way across was this service 381 to Edinburgh driven by Bobby Brown, who had the affectionate nickname of 'Paw Broon'. It ran across in conjunction with this small bus, which was bought down from Kerr's Miniature Railway, Arbroath, for this ceremonial occasion. (*Bobby Brown Jnr*)

In this photograph, an unknown Bristol FS6G Lodekka is seen at Kelty Cross on a local service to Kirkcaldy. As can be seen in an earlier photograph, this area was the terminus for the tram service on the short stretch of line that branched off at Kelty Junction in Cowdenbeath. Kelty bus depot was behind the photographer on that side of the road. (*Claire Pendrous*)

Northern Counties-bodied Albion Lowlander UCS 616 (FRE26) makes its exit from Pilmuir Street, Dunfermline, and turns into Carnegie Street, which would soon become Carnegie Drive when the dual carriageway in this area was built. The building on the right-hand corner, formerly a public baths, would soon disappear too. (*Robert Dickson Collection*)

It is my opinion that the early version of the coach livery, with the roofs painted red, was just a wee bit too over-powering. Readers may wish to make their own opinion as they look at AXA 219A (FAC19), an Alexander Y-type-bodied AEC Reliance, pictured here at Dunfermline depot on 23 August 1963, two months after its arrival when new. (*John Sinclair*)

Pictured at rest, and gleaming in the midday sun, we have on the left KMS 493 (FPD124), a Leyland PSUC1/2 from 1958 with Alexander body work, and on the right GMS 414 (FGA4), a 1955 Guy Arab LUF, again with body work by Alexander. I have noticed many times how clean the buses always looked when under Alexander's wing. This image would be dated to around the end of the 1960s. (*John Sinclair*)

Fife operated five Albion Aberdonian buses, all with Alexander's own bodywork, which arrived new in the Kingdom in 1958. KWG 585 (FNL10) was based at Lochgelly depot, and is the only example I have seen wearing coach livery. It would be withdrawn in 1974 along with its three remaining counterparts, FNL13 having been withdrawn the previous year, and was broken up by Alexander (Fife) for spare parts. Although only five were operated in Fife, the fleet number sequence was inherited from the days before the 1961 split. NL1–9 were operated by Alexander (Northern). (*John Sinclair*)

This is DWG 772 (FPC39), a Leyland PSU1/15 with Alexander bodywork. It was just one of these vehicles allocated to Dunfermline depot, where it is seen in this photograph. When these vehicles were built in 1952, they had this central door arrangement, which was a suitable arrangement for that particular era. (*John Sinclair*)

EMS 170 (FPC52) was from the batch delivered the following year (1953), again with Alexander bodywork. In 1965, a number of these vehicles were converted to forward entrance and the result is seen here, again, within the confines of Dunfermline depot. This aided operational needs in the 1960s, as the population was growing and buses were becoming busier, when operated by the driver only (OMO – One Man Operated). (*John Sinclair*)

AMS 317 (FRO542), a 1945 Guy Arab 2 with Weymann bodywork, is caught entering its home depot in Lochgelly, no doubt after a long and hard day out on the road. As in the photograph of this bus wearing blue livery earlier on, the ribbed effect of the Weymann roof panelling is seen to good effect. (*John Sinclair*)

An Alexander-bodied Guy Arab LUF, GMS 416 (FGA6), is seen between duties, parked up at its home depot of Kelty. New in 1955, this vehicle made its final journey from Kelty to Muir's in Kirkcaldy in 1971. The raised fuel tank was a prominent feature at Kelty depot. (*John Sinclair*)

One of the Alexander-bodied Guy Arab LUFs allocated to Lochgelly depot was GMS 413 (FGA3). It is seen without the red roof, but the tinted front sky lights are quite prominent here and cover the driver in a strange pink hue. Again, it is worth noticing the cleanliness of a vehicle which is practically all cream in colour. (*John Sinclair*)

Another image of a Craven-bodied Guy Arab 3, AWG386 (FRO600), shown here at Dunfermline depot, to illustrate the curved rear windows on both the upper and lower saloons. They were a prominent feature of the Cravens body style, on both decks, and both sides of double decked buses. FRO600 was withdrawn in 1970 when it was twenty-two years old and sold to a dealer in Preston. (*Mike Penn*)

MWG 364 (FPD149), an Alexander-bodied Leyland PSUC1/2 from 1959, catches a moment's rest while working on service 44B between Saline and Dunfermline Carnegie Drive bus station. This service also takes in Wellwood, to the north of the town, Redcraigs Toll, Upper Steelend and Steelend turning circle. This bus was withdrawn and sold to Muir's in 1975. (*John Sinclair*)

Seen parked up at the rear of Dunfermline Carnegie Drive bus station, we find BMS 590 (FG68), a single-deck Guy Arab 3 with the unique style of Massey bodywork. The nearside mirror must have been quite awkward at times, as it seems they were located slightly to the rear of the driver's side view. (*Paul Redmond*)

AEC Reliance 7429 SP (FAC9), one of the first twelve to arrive in Fife in 1962, is seen in a quiet corner at Dunfermline depot in the mid-1960s. It lasted until it was withdrawn and scrapped in 1977 at Muir's. The large grey building in the background was, if I remember, a part of the gasworks near the rear of the depot. The author unfortunately can't recall the purpose of the small glazed panel behind the front wheel arch. (*John Sinclair*)

This was Kelty depot's Leyland PSU1/2, EMS 167 (FPC49). It was, of course, bodied by Alexander, with the centrally positioned entrance door. This was one of the Leyland vehicles not to receive a re-positioned entrance door. (*John Sinclair*)

FGM 30 (FRE23) was a Northern Counties-bodied Albion Lowlander, acquired from Central SMT in 1965 when only two years old. It is seen travelling down Dunfermline's New Row, past the Alhambra, which by this time was in use as a bingo hall, on a local service 1 from Beatty Place, just off Robertson Road, to Linburn Road at the east side of the Abbeyview estate. (*Mike Penn*)

Another run on the service 1 seen in the charge of FLF Lodekka HXA 404E (FRD204) as it makes its way past the railway viaduct at Bothwell Street. The viaduct is about all that remains in the photograph as the New Row is now truncated beyond the bridge. The rear of the now-demolished Brig Tavern can be seen under the left-hand arch, and the large chimney, a part of the former Dunfermline and West Fife Hospital, is now gone also. (*Mike Penn*)

Cowdenbeath depot is the location of these two 1945 Guy Arab 2s, both with Northern Counties bodywork, but curiously differing in various areas of the panelling. AMS 211 (FRO504), on the left, ended up as a training vehicle in 1967 and can be seen on page 93 of *Fife Buses*. AMS 312 (FRO537) was withdrawn and sold to Muir's for scrapping in 1967. A withdrawn Albion Victor, painted grey, can be seen to the left of these Guy Arabs, also awaiting disposal. (*John Sinclair*)

A fantastic broadside view of EGM 7 (FRE9), one of the eighteen Northern Counties-bodied Albion Lowlanders that came to Alexander (Fife) in 1965 from Central SMT, in exchange for fourteen new FLF Lodekkas. It shows the application of the Fife logo, along with the Central SMT livery it was still wearing, when photographed on 22 April 1965 at the turning area in Carnegie Drive bus stance. (*John Sinclair*)

UCS 614 (FRE30) was one of fourteen Northern Counties-bodied Albion Lowlander buses that came to Fife around 1966 from Western SMT. Although not the best looking of buses, no one can deny that they did their job, even though some of them were painted in a rather plain-looking livery, as pictured here. In the background, the offices and works of Erskine Beverage can be seen beyond the 'Fine Fare' car park. The area is still instantly recognisable when compared to how it looks today. (*John Sinclair*)

AXA 219A (FAC19) was an Alexander Y-type-bodied AEC Reliance. It was one of fourteen delivered in 1963, and is seen here at Dunfermline depot, not long after delivery, wearing the original configuration of coach livery with the red roof. By the end of the decade, the red roofs were repainted cream. A Massey-bodied Guy Arab 3, still in blue livery, can be seen peaking out of the shed door on the left. (*John Sinclair*)

The end of 1965 saw the arrival of the Albion Viking to the Fife fleet. Twelve arrived that year, and DXA 409C (FNV9) was one of the vehicles allocated to Dunfermline's depot. It was still going strong when photographed ten years later, on 13 August 1975, while working a local service to Rumblingwell from Rosyth. (*John Sinclair*)

FXA 713D (FNV13) was one of the 1966 intake of Albion Viking buses. These had bodies by Alexander's Northern Ireland offshoot, Potters of Belfast. This one is parked up by the fuel pump at Dunfermline depot, again on 13 August 1975, but is getting ready to get underway to take up its next tour of duty. The building in the background was a part of the now-demolished old Dunfermline High School. (*John Sinclair*)

This photograph was taken on 13 August 1975, the same time as the image of FRE30 a couple of pages back. This is the area at Dunfermline depot where the driver changeovers occur, adjacent to 'the wee Asda'. None of the houses shown here now exist, either at the bus stop or further up the road, where the present Bank of Scotland building now stands. As seen from most viewpoints within Dunfermline, the Abbey dominates the skyline of the town centre. (*John Sinclair*)

Passing by Dunfermline Fire Station on 8 April 1972 is Daimler Fleetline SXA 68K (FRF68). This was one of five with Northern Counties bodywork that arrived new in 1971, but which were deemed to be non-standard, all five being subsequently moved on to Alexander (Midland) by the end of October 1975. How quiet the roads were 40 years ago! (*John Sinclair*)

Photographed on 31 July 1975, when only 6 months old, HSF 549N (FT4) was one of ten Ford chassis with forty-five-seat coach bodywork by Duple, seen inside its home depot of Dunfermline. The Ford chassis wasn't ideally suited to the needs of Fife's services, and this vehicle was one of five Duple vehicles that went to Highland Omnibuses in 1979, the other five moving to Northern. (*John Sinclair*)

A rather fine image taken in Cowdenbeath depot, which has been included to illustrate the variations in livery application, even on vehicles of the same type. Four Albion Lowlanders are seen here in a mixture of body styles and cream relief bands and lining. A little bit of variety kept the subject matter interesting. (*John Sinclair*)

PXA 638J (FRF38) was an Eastern Coach Works-bodied Daimler Fleetline, new to Alexander (Fife) in 1971. They were quite distinguishable from other Fleetlines with their white/cream window rubbers which was a feature of ECW-built vehicles of the era. FRF38 is seen here awaiting its next turn of duty while parked up just outside its home depot at Lochgelly on 8 April 1972. (*John Sinclair*)

This fantastic image shows the rear end of a couple of Alexander-bodied Albion Vikings in one of the sheds at Dunfermline's St Leonards Street depot. On the left we see DXA 411C (FNV11), while on the right is DXA 409C (FNV9), with a great view of a makeshift arrangement to improve engine cooling on these vehicles. (*John Sinclair*)

A rather atmospheric image of RWG 370 (FRD147), an LD6G type Lodekka from 1961, as it sits beside the wall on the entry road into the depot at Dunfermline. On the other side of this wall is St Leonards Primary School, which has stood on this site for the last 110 years. This image can be dated to late 1969 or the early 1970s as there is a Daimler Fleetline engine bustle on view, as well as the cream relief bands appearing with black lining. (*Robert Dickson Collection*)

Taken just inside the depot yard, further in from the previous photograph, we find two of the recently new Mk 1 Ailsa buses that Fife began purchasing in large numbers from 1975 onwards. They were like a breath of fresh air when they were introduced, with their high bridge body work, peaked front and rear domes, and the distinctive whine of the small turbocharged front engine. (*Brian Pritchard*)

Mk 1 Ailsa KSF 4N (FRA4) was only just over a month old when photographed in Dunfermline's St Leonards Street on 31 August 1975. It is seen on local Dunfermline town service 1, which ran between Linburn Road, to the east of the Abbeyview estate, and Beatty Place, just off Robertson Road on the main road up to Townhill. The houses on the other side of the road were eventually all knocked down to make way for road widening in the 1990s. (*John Sinclair*)

Mk 2 Ailsa OSC 57V (FRA57) sits in the bus stop lay-by outside the 'Fine Fare' superstore at St Leonards, Dunfermline. This is adjacent to the bus depot, which was behind a row of houses on the opposite side of the street. A driver changeover has just taken place before the bus will continue on the ever-busy route to Rosyth Dockyard. (*Robert Dickson*)

Dunfermline-based Mk 1 Ailsa UFS 876R (FRA43) is seen further up the coast in Kirkcaldy on a service 306 from Upper Largo. It has just left Kirkcaldy bus station and is heading down to the promenade on the second half of its run back to the 'Auld Grey Town'. It wore this special white 'Landmark' livery for a short while and was known to Dunfermline depot staff as 'The Ghost'.

The Carnegie Drive bus stance was not a large area by any means, and as a result it always looked very busy, as seen here on a typical day in the early 1980s. Although it was situated on the main road into the town from the west, there was always ample time for passengers to cross the road, as well as enough room for buses manoeuvring into, and out of, the bus station. (*Jo Freeman/Dunfermline Photos*)

YSF 74S (FPE74) is seen here employed on a typical duty for the Leyland Leopard. Service 80 was a demanding run from Dunfermline Carnegie Drive bus station to North Queensferry via Rosyth Middlebank Street and Inverkeithing High Street. The road layout has changed in this location to accommodate the (eventual) building of a new superstore where the Carnegie Drive bus station once stood. (*Paul Redmond*)

An interesting photograph showing the inside of shed number 2 at Dunfermline depot. On show are two Leyland Leopards, a Daimler Fleetline, a tow wagon and two Alexander-bodied AEC Reliances including AXA 221A (FAC21), as seen here. Number 2 shed was the last to be built at Dunfermline, shown by the straight roof girders compared to the curved girders seen in shed 3 to the right of the AEC. (*John Sinclair*)

Another scene in Dunfermline that would change quite radically due to road improvements is this area between the 'Fine Fare' superstore, which was on the right of the picture, and the bus depot, which is behind the row of houses on the left. KSF 3N (FRA3) can be seen on 31 July 1975 on a local service 1 between Linburn Road and Beatty Place. (*John Sinclair*)

One of the Mk 1 Ailsa buses of Dunfermline depot turns into Carnegie Drive from Pilmuir Street, having come down on a service 75 from Wellwood at the northern extreme of Dunfermline. LSX 24P (FRA24) is wearing the short-lived experimental livery, but retains the 'F' prefix letter to the fleet number. The now-derelict textile factory can be seen clearly in the background. (*Paul Redmond*)

Another Mk 1 Ailsa, OSC 49V (FRA49), works its way around the junction/roundabout that was situated at the bottom of the New Row. There was a public house, The Brig Tavern, behind the photographer on this 'roundabout' that the author used to visit on a Friday afternoon after the dockyard dayshift finished. The tenement at the rear end of the bus also disappeared when the roads were improved in this area in the 1990s. (*Paul Redmond*)

Nothing has changed in the thirty-odd years since this photograph was taken, with the exception of the road vehicles. OSC 52V (FRA52) was a Mk 2 Ailsa with the raised driving position and windscreen, and is seen on a local service 77 to Rosyth Dockyard, a journey the author made many times while working in the establishment as a fitter/turner. (*Paul Redmond*)

Another Mk 2 Ailsa, OSC 53V (FRA53), works its way down the New Row in another scene that is instantly recognisable today. It will be noted that the Ailsa buses were extensively used on the popular service 77 to and from Rosyth Dockyard, and it was on this run that the author's sister met her husband while working together as conductress and driver. (*Paul Redmond*)

JXA 930F (FE30), an Eastern Coach Works-bodied Bristol RELL, undergoes a headlamp change in the yard at Dunfermline depot. The off-side access panel can be seen against the side of the vehicle for easy access for the engineering staff. Dunfermline never really had its own RELL buses, only getting one now and again as a result of vehicle movements within the Fife Company. (*Clive A. Brown*)

An interloper is seen here in the shape of Kirkcaldy depot's Leyland Leopard WFS 143W (FPE143). It is passing the entrance to Dunfermline depot, which is on the right of the picture, while a female inspector can be seen at the front of the vehicle. The houses on the opposite side of the road were all demolished to make way for road improvements in the 1990s. (*Robert Dickson*)

Another Leyland Leopard on another run from Leven is seen making light work of the run up Dunfermline's New Row. CSF 164W (FPE164) would not look out of place running up the New Row today, as it is one of the areas not to have been changed or altered by any road improvements or building work. The car driver on the extreme right seems rather impatient as he tries to squeeze his way out in front of other road users. (*Paul Redmond*)

By the end of the 1970s, the humble Daimler Fleetline found itself relegated to more mundane duties such as the local school runs and workers' services. Not that they were unreliable or anything, they were just 'ousted' by the more robust Ailsa bus. This selection of Alexander-bodied Fleetlines, including NXA 624H (FRF24), is parked up at the rear of Dunfermline depot awaiting their next duties. (*Clive A. Brown*)

Two of Dunfermline's early Y-type Leopard coaches, OXA 454H (FPE4) and OXA 456H (FPE6), sit in the sun at their home depot at St Leonards. FPE4 had just completed a journey up and down the coast between Dunfermline and Upper Largo on the 306/310 service. I believe the bus would have travelled up as a service 306, and returned as service 310. I do not think that the corporate image logo suited the coach livery, but that is just my opinion. (*John Sinclair*)

The Leyland Leopard with Duple body work was a good combination, well suited to inter-urban work, as shown here with CFS 117S (FPE117). It is seen climbing the steep New Row in Dunfermline as it nears the end of its journey from Leven on a service 7A. This particular vehicle has the Mk 1 version of the Duple body with the shallow windscreen. (*Paul Redmond*)

By comparison, GSG 125T (FPE125) had the alternative Mk 2 version of Duple body work, distinguishable by the deeper windscreen. The two versions were basically the same body shell, with no other differences. FPE125 is seen within the confines of Dunfermline Carnegie Drive bus station, having just arrived on a service 78 from Saline via Redcraigs. (*Robert Dickson*)

Remember what it was like before Dunfermline High Street was pedestrianised? Here we find XXA 854M (FPE54) making its way up the High Street on a local service 71, which at the time, in the early 1980s, was a Townhill–Abbeyview–Woodmill circular service. It is being closely followed by another Leyland Leopard, heading for Leven. This bus was eventually converted into a tow wagon, and is now preserved at the Scottish Vintage Bus Museum at Lathalmond near Dunfermline. (*Robert Dickson*)

One of Cowdenbeath depot's 11.6-metre Mk 2 Leyland Nationals, RSG 821V (FPN21), is caught passing Dunfermline Fire Station as it nears its terminus at the bus station next door. I have included this image as it shows to good effect the rippled effect of the side roof panels caused by the riveting. This is quite normal, but it is only noticeable when conditions are right regarding angle of the sunlight. (*Robert Dickson*)

RXA 52J (RF52) has just had a recent re-paint into the new, non-standard livery in this photograph taken inside Lochgelly Depot on 3 April 1981. Lochgelly depot closed its doors for the last time a year later, with the workload, and vehicles, being transferred to Cowdenbeath and Kirkcaldy depots. (*John Sinclair*)

Another photograph of RXA 52J (RF52) sees it just having left Lochgelly depot, and about to start a part run to the village of Ballingry, the terminus for the popular service 19 from Dunfermline. Again, it is wearing the non-standard livery applied to various Fleetlines and Ailsa buses around the start of the 1980s. Vehicles in this livery had the 'F' prefix on the fleet number removed. (*John Sinclair*)

Alexander-bodied Leyland Leopard CSF 164W (FPE164) heads out of the bus station in Carnegie Drive, Dunfermline, about to embark on the second leg of its journey from Edinburgh to Perth. When standing in this position today, everything looks exactly the same as in this photograph. Stand on the other side of the road, as in the next image, and it is a completely different story. The old fire station is still there, but the bus station has been consigned to history. (*Robert Dickson*)

Seen here on 3 April 1981, a trio of Alexander-bodied Daimler Fleetlines are depicted wearing the experimental large logo livery as applied to certain double-decked vehicles in the early 1980s. Among them, in the centre of the photograph, is SXA 65K (RF65), of 1971 vintage, which eventually ended up in the fleet of Rapsons of Inverness. (*John Sinclair*)

Low railway bridges and high bridge bodies don't work well together, as depicted in this image of LSX 25P (FRA25), a 1975 Ailsa Mk 1 with Alexander bodywork. It is pictured in one of the sheds at Dunfermline depot in the early 1980s after striking the railway bridge at the end of Woodmill Street, before the roadwork was altered in this area. The bus was repaired and is known to have lasted into the 'Large Logo' era.

A fine image showing one of Dunfermline's Leyland Leopards negotiating the roundabout at the Bothwell Street/Netherton Broad Street junction. Although not seen in the photograph, the Brig Tavern public house sat on this 'roundabout' at the bottom of the New Row. Also, as can be seen through the arches, it is noticeable that this is before Bothwell Street was widened. The height of the tower at St Leonard's church is seen to good effect here too. (*Jo Freeman/Dunfermline Photos*)

One of the Leyland Leopards to operate with Rennies of Dunfermline was this Plaxton-bodied version. New in 1976 to Southdown as their 1268, it was acquired by Rennies in 1987 and it spent seven years there before moving on to Gibson of Moffat. It is seen here in its former home depot at Cairneyhill. (*Gary Seamarks*)

Passing the entrance to the Fife Scottish bus depot at St Leonards in Dunfermline, we find East Lancs-bodied Dennis Dominator LFR 131T, a former Blackburn machine new in 1979 as their fleet number 131. It was acquired by Rennies in 1986 and is seen on a local run to Saline, a village to the north-east of Dunfermline. (*Gary Seamarks*)

RKA 436N was a Scania Metropolitan with MCW body work which was new in 1974 to Merseyside PTE as their fleet number 4036. It then had a stint with Hull Corporation before arriving at Rennies in 1987. It is seen on a local service to Inverkeithing in this image, taken in Dunfermline Market Street bus station, which is fully occupied here by 'interlopers'. (*Gary Seamarks*)

Still wearing the livery and fleet name of its former owner, Blackburn, we see JFR 402N, a Leyland Atlantean with East Lancs body work, departing from Market Street and heading for Hillend Industrial Estate at Dalgety Bay in May 1988. No one could deny the variety of vehicles operated by Rennies during the 1980s, when they were competing with Fife Scottish on various local services. (*Gary Seamarks*)

Two of the Leyland Atlanteans acquired by Rennies from Strathclyde PTE in 1988 are seen resting in the layover area at Market Street in Dunfermline. The vehicle on the right is still in the livery of its former owners, but the fleet name on the front of the vehicle has been rather crudely painted over. It was eventually painted in Rennies' own livery shortly afterwards. (*Gordon Stirling*)

The former entrance to Market Street from Carnegie Drive is the location here, as we find this Mk 2 Leyland National on a local service 71 between James Street and Garvock Bank, an estate to the east of the town. A short length of Market Street still exists here, albeit used as a service road for the extended Kingsgate Centre. The buildings in the background, including the Carnegie Clinic, are still there, although the road layout has changed rather significantly (for the worse). (*Robert Dickson*)

Suitably framed by the adjacent foliage, Volvo Citybus C793 USG (FRA93) sits at the unofficial pick up/drop off area near stance 1 of the old Market Street bus station. It was on show, displaying colours thought at the time to be close to those used by the old Dunfermline & District Traction Company.

A typical image that could have been taken in any depot yard in Fife under Scottish Bus Group ownership. The Volvo Ailsa Mk 1 and 2 were the main double-decker types in the Kingdom and more than earned their keep. This photograph was taken at Cowdenbeath and the Ailsas, all wearing the large logo livery, are in the company of a solitary Citybus.

The entrance to Market Street in Dunfermline still exists, although it is now merely a service road for the extended Kingsgate shopping centre. A Volvo Citybus, an Alexander 'PS'-bodied Volvo B10 and an Ailsa Mk 1 are seen at this often busy junction, all keeping uniformity with the large logo livery. (*Christopher Leach*)

HSC113T (313) was an 11.3-metre-long Leyland National Mk 1 with a roof-mounted heater pod. This was one of the first thirteen to be operated by Fife Scottish when they arrived in 1978, and can be seen within the confines of the engineering workshops at Dunfermline depot. (*Kenneth Barclay*)

The late 1980s saw the arrival of several Leyland National Mk 2s from both Northern and Highland Omnibuses. WAS 765V (365) was one of the buses that came via Highland and was used primarily on the service 19 between Ballingry and Dunfermline.

A pair of big cats is spotted lurking in the depths at Cowdenbeath depot! On the left is Leyland Tiger B209 FFS (509) with Alexander 'TC'-type bodywork, while Leyland Leopard CFS 115S (215) with Duple Dominant Mk 1 bodywork is seen on the right.

The first of five images showing the various wrap-around adverts applied to Leyland Leopards during the 1980s. This Leopard is YSF 93S (FPE93) and carries an advert for Euroscot, a local franchise that apparently sold Alfa Romeo cars. (*Robert Dickson*)

CSF 162W (FPE162) is captured within the confines of Kinross, near the popular Bridgend Hotel. It is making its way back to Edinburgh on a long journey from Perth, although it was not an unpleasant journey. This Leopard carries an advert for House of Hair, located in Edinburgh's West End. (*Robert Dickson*)

Our third offering shows CSF 163W (PE163) leaving Carnegie Drive bus station in Dunfermline on a service 56 run to Edinburgh. This one wears a wrap-around advert for another car dealership. Laidlaw was a major car dealer and specialised in selling Ford vehicles. (*Robert Dickson*)

Leyland Leopard WFS 135W (PE135) is seen in St Leonards Street, Dunfermline, between the Fife Scottish bus depot and Fine Fare superstore. It is seen wearing an in-house wrap-around advert displaying the price for a return journey between Dunfermline and London. The bus is on a part route working to Dalgety Bay on the service 7A. (*Robert Dickson*)

Another wrap-around advert for the Laidlaw car franchise, as carried by XSG 71R (PE71). Not as bold as the advert carried by PE163, but with a little bit more colour. This Leopard is seen at the turning area behind Carnegie Drive bus station and, again like PE163, is on a service 56 to Edinburgh. (*Robert Dickson*)

Cowdenbeath depot is the location as we see a trio of Alexander-bodied Leyland Leopards. They all carry the 'Large Logo' livery which, I believe, enhanced the look of the body style of the Leopard.

Photographed from a raised vantage point, we see one of Dunfermline depot's Leyland Atlantean buses with Alexander AL-type bodywork. In May 1984, Fife Scottish bought ten of these vehicles from Grampian Regional Transport, and although they were dual-doored, they were quickly converted to single-door use.

Alexander-bodied Daimler Fleetline XXA 373M (1073) is at rest at the rear of its home depot in Dunfermline. Formerly FRF73, it enjoyed retirement in its new-found role as the training vehicle for Dunfermline. The yellow livery applied makes a remarkable comparison to the colour used by sister company Northern Scottish, another former Walter Alexander company. (*Kenneth Barclay*)

Just before privatisation in the early 1990s, the fledgling Stagecoach company used Dunfermline bus station on many of its long distance runs. 2412 SC was a single-deck Neoplan and is seen entering the old Market Street bus station in June 1988. Little did we know that just over three years later, these colours would be seen a lot more when Stagecoach would buy the Fife Scottish bus company in 1991. (*Gary Seamarks*)

About 1996, there was competition from Firstbus on the routes between Ballingry and Dunfermline, with some journeys extending to Edinburgh. I believe this was retaliation by First Group for the X25/X15 services that run between Glasgow and Cumbernauld. P505 XSH (505) was a Scania with 'Wright Axcess Ultralow' bodywork and is seen at the terminus in Ballingry. (*Suzy Scott*)

Another view of P505 XSH (505), taken in Lochgelly on a lovely day in 1997, seen on a run from Ballingry to Dunfermline. Although not shown on this vehicle, Fife-based First Group vehicles were branded as 'FifeFirst'. (*Suzy Scott*)

Allison's provided a little bit of competition for Stagecoach at the end of the 1990s. By the time of the new millennium, Stagecoach had removed this competition by buying them out. They had a small depot at Linburn Industrial Estate in Dunfermline, but had previously been located near 'Back of Muir' and at Waulkmill Farm, near Crombie. This image shows two of the Leyland National Mk 1s used by Allison's before being bought out by Stagecoach. (*Suzy Scott*)

Stagecoach had not long owned Fife Scottish when it tried out this experimental fleet name on Volvo Citybus C787 USG (987). It was quite a bold style and one I believe suited the Stagecoach livery at the time. Nothing ever came of it, though, and it was replaced with the more mundane Stagecoach combined fleet name and logo. This bus is seen on Carnegie Drive, adjacent to Dunfermline Sheriff Court, on a local town service. (*David Love*)

RSG 821V (321) is seen here, sitting in the yard at its home depot of Cowdenbeath. New in 1979, it was an 11.6-metre Mk 2 Leyland National with no roof-mounted heater pod. It does, however, carry a modification to the engine air cooling system that can be seen at the rear of the vehicle.

Between 1993/4, Stagecoach acquired a number of Volvo B6 chassis with Alexander Dash bodywork from Ribble buses, another Stagecoach-owned operator down south. M670 SSX (670) makes its way down Dunfermline's New Row en route to Pitcorthie, an estate to the south of the town, on the circular D4 service. The service ran via the King Malcolm Hotel and returned via Aberdour Road. There was also a D3 service which ran the reverse route around Pitcorthie. The B6s were quite prone to blowing their turbochargers, perhaps a result of the hard work climbing Dunfermline's many hills. (*John Law*)

Bought in large numbers by Stagecoach as the main vehicle type for their express network of services, the Volvo B10M interurban coach with Plaxton bodywork did sterling work for the Fife company. When spare coaches were available, they were often used on runs like the popular 55 service between Edinburgh and Dunfermline/Perth, as seen here with M946 TSX (546). (*Barry Sanjana*)

Volvo B10 R337 HFS (20337) with Alexander 'PS' bodywork is taking on passengers in the old Market Street bus station in Dunfermline on 17 May 2003. It is on the local service 74 to Blairhall, which was the type of inter-urban route that was most suitable for these vehicles. It carries an all-over advert for local radio station Kingdom FM. Because of its colour, this particular vehicle was known to drivers as 'The Stealth'. (*Suzy Scott*)

Alexander RL-bodied Volvo Olympian J807 WFS (707) is seen in Dunfermline James Street in the summer of 2002 on a local service. As can be seen, the destination display equipment was not working, as happened often with the 'Hanover' display units, resulting in the route number being crudely written on the paper stuck to the inside of the windscreen. (*Suzy Scott*)

The Dennis Dart with Alexander Dash bodywork – not one of my favourite buses. They were prone to jumping between gears when driving around town, resulting in a very uncomfortable drive for passengers and driver alike. This example, N306 AMC (682), is pictured in Dunfermline's James Street on a local D9 service between the Queen Margaret Hospital and Abbeyview. One of the newer Alexander ALX200 Darts can be seen at the rear of 682 in this photograph, taken around the turn of the millennium. (*Suzy Scott*)

Around 2003, there were a lot of bus movements between the various Stagecoach operations. Fife had acquired a number of ex-London, Northern Counties-bodied Volvo Olympians with dual doors, of which R158 HHK (16158) was an example, to replace a number of Alexander-bodied examples which had been moved on. These vehicles were quickly put in service in the condition they arrived in, but over the coming months, they each had the central doors removed and were repainted into the standard Stagecoach livery. This example is seen entering Market Street bus station in Dunfermline while on a local service between Dunfermline and Blairhall. (*Suzy Scott*)

P975 UBV (575) was one of the Plaxton-bodied, articulated Volvo B10 coaches of Dunfermline depot, used on the X15/X25 services between Glasgow and Cumbernauld. They operated with 'Hostesses' who issued tickets with wayfarer machines, and supplied passengers with refreshments. The author worked on these services for a while, and met his future wife while doing so. Firstbus retaliated by starting the 56 service in Fife between Ballingry and Dunfermline. (*Innes Cameron*)

Volvo Citybus C792 USG (15292) wears the Stagecoach 'whoosh' style of livery in this view taken on 17 May 2003. The bus was sitting waiting on another vehicle to vacate the allotted stance for that service (I know this as I was the driver of the bus in the image). The location is James Street, the starting point for most of the local town services at the time. (*Suzy Scott*)

Initially, the Alexander ALX300-bodied MAN chassis vehicles bought by Stagecoach around 1999 were used on the popular 19 service between Ballingry and its new route extension to Rosyth Dockyard. SP06 DBY (22406) is seen just leaving Ballingry terminus in the colours applied to commemorate the 100th anniversary of the route between Dunfermline and Cowdenbeath. (*Robert Clark*)

The north end of Edinburgh's North Bridge was at one time the starting point for the evening return journey on the service X52 to Townhill. N316 VMS (316) is an Alexander PS-bodied Volvo B10, and will make its way to George Street via Surgeons Hall and The Mound in this image taken in June 2002. (*Suzy Scott*)

Stagecoach Fife had a brief relationship with the Leyland Titan in the early part of the new millennium. NUW 605Y (742) was an all-Leyland vehicle, still with dual doors from its London days, and is seen sitting in the bus layover area at Ferrytoll Park and Ride on 25 June 2002. It was being used on shuttle duties that afternoon between Ferrytoll and Dalgety Bay. The second exit was made inoperable by the use of a steel bar riveted across both leafs of the door. (*Suzy Scott*)

A beautiful day during July 2002 sees Alexander Dash-bodied Volvo B6 L658 HKS (658) waiting to depart on a local D2 service back to James Street from the new Tesco superstore at Dulloch Park in Dunfermline. Dunfermline's town centre services changed radically at this time due to the ever-growing eastern expansion known as 'DEX'. The photographer has once again managed to capture 'yours truly' behind the wheel. (*Suzy Scott*)

During 2005, Stagecoach briefly owned ten Scania double-decked buses obtained from Busways of Newcastle, with Alexander's' RH type of bodywork. H430 BNL (15310) is seen heading through Cowdenbeath High Street, having previously completed a local school run. All ten buses never lasted long and were all subsequently moved on to other operators or disposed of. (*Robert Clark*)

One of the thirteen Mercedes-Benz Vito 110CD Traveliners that were used by Stagecoach in the brief venture that was 'Yellow Taxibus'. Launched in August 2003 as 'a new cost-effective model for demand responsive transport', the Yellow Taxibus experiment never achieved commercial viability. What it did show was that it could have potential, with the help of modest public sector funding. (*Donald Stewart*)

New in 2006, the Optare Solo was a versatile vehicle that could tackle any service within its range. They were suited to the demanding town services within Dunfermline, as seen in this photograph of SP06 FNE (47368) at Townhill turning circle. Two or three were converted for use on the new airport service from Inverkeithing to Edinburgh, but this often suffered from overcrowding. Like most modern buses, they now suffer with gearbox problems. They just don't make them like they used to!

Parked up within Dunfermline depot, Alexander Dennis Trident SP05 EKY (34726) awaits its first turn of duty for the day. These vehicles were new in July 2005 and were employed on both the service 78 to High Valleyfield and the local town services D5/D6. Much suited for running around the hills of Dunfermline, for some reason, they were all moved on to other Fife depots.

The Dennis Trident is one of those vehicles you either love or hate to drive. They seem to labour unnecessarily at times, and as they get older, they tend to jump up and down between gears a lot. SP04 DCX (18100) is pictured at Pentland Rise in Dalgety Bay, waiting to start an early-morning short run to Dunfermline on the service 7.

K721 ASC (14721) was one of the first batches of Leyland Olympians ordered by the new Stagecoach Fife company in June 1992. They had Alexander's low-height RL type of bodywork, and many were stationed at Cowdenbeath. This was one such vehicle, and is seen in Cowdenbeath High Street, working on a service 16 to Kirkcaldy. (*Robert Clark*)

Hiding in the shed at Dunfermline is SP06 FVA (53248), one of the B7R coaches with Plaxton bodywork employed on express service work throughout Fife. They are fitted with wheelchair access lifts which, by all accounts, are prone to jamming in a lowered position, rendering the vehicle unserviceable. They don't appear to have the popularity among drivers that the B10s seemed to enjoy.

Nearest the camera, we see SP59 AOV (19545), one of the Enviro 400 double-deckers from Alexander Dennis. These buses are basically newer, greener versions of the Dennis Trident buses still used throughout Fife. They have 'one piece' front windows on both decks, which must prove costly to replace in case of accident. It is pictured in the yard at Dunfermline, in the company of two training vehicles in different liveries.

SP59CTU (27606) represents the style now used by Alexander Dennis for single-deck vehicles. This is one of the Enviro 300s belonging to Dunfermline depot and is photographed parked up at the waste ground beside Ferrytoll Park and Ride, Inverkeithing. A versatile type of vehicle much suited for inter urban type of service runs.

This recent image shows Northern Counties-bodied Volvo Olympian R172 HHK (16172) about to enter the new bus station in Dunfermline, situated off Pilmuir Street and located at the rear of the city's Post Office. It is found on a local service 74 to Blairhall, its usual type of route, but comes off mid-afternoon to do school runs. (*John Carter*)

Negotiating its way around the corner between Carnegie Drive and Pilmuir Street, we find Scania Omnilink SP57 CNU (24007) being closely followed by one of Stagecoach's older PS types. Nine of these vehicles arrived around 2008 for use on the busy Dunfermline/Dalgety Bay to Edinburgh services. Great care has to be taken at this busy corner due to the abundance of 'street furniture' in the vicinity. (*John Carter*)

Bringing us up to date is SP62 BKN (54109), one of the new tri-axle Volvo B13 buses for use on the comprehensive express network operated by Stagecoach Fife. This is one of nine delivered to Dunfermline depot in November 2012, and is seen in the capable hands of one of the depot supervisors.